Zoot Suit Riots:

Clothes, Culture, and Murder

by Barbara J. Turner

Illustrations by Lisa Greenleaf

For Mur: It wouldn't have happened without you. ~Barbara T.

To Bob, Meghan & Chris: Thank you for believing in me and letting me shine. ~Lisa G.

Apprentice Shop Books, LLC
Amherst, New Hampshire

Text copyright ©2015

For information regarding permissions contact:
   Apprentice Shop Books, LLC
   Box 375
   Amherst, NH 03031
   www.apprenticeshopbooks.com

LIBRARY OF CONGRESS CATALOGING-IN-PUBLICATION DATA

Turner, Barbara J.
   Zoot Suit Riots: Clothes, Culture, and Murder ; Illustrations by Lisa Greenleaf
   p.cm. – Once, in America Series
   Includes glossary and index
   1. Zoot Suit Riots—History—the 1940s—juvenile literature.

ISBN-13: 978-09842549-3-4

Printed in United States of America

 Cover design, illustrations, and book design by Lisa Greenleaf
Greenleaf Design Studio www.Lisagreenleaf.com

Table of Contents:

Chapter 1: José Gallardo Diaz 5

Chapter 2: The Road To Ruin 15

Chapter 3: The Sleepy Lagoon Murder Trial 29

Chapter 4: Riot! 37

Chapter 5: Freedom? 51

The Zoot Suit Riots Influence the Arts 62

Across the Nation 66

What About Today? 68

Timeline 70

Glossary 72

Index 74

Photo/Illustration Credits 77

About the Author and Illustrator 79

Zoot Suit Summary 80

Once, in America. . .

. . . *zoot suits were all the rage among young men.*
But, if you happened to be wearing one in Los Angeles,
California, during the summer of 1943, you might have
ended up in jail. You might have ended up beaten or dead.

    For wearing a suit.

    A zoot suit.

Chapter 1:
José Gallardo Diaz

Cool Cats

Jazz! By the early 1940s, it was the coolest thing on the American music scene. 'Swing' was the thing and jazz clubs were jumping. They blared with the big band sounds of Benny Goodman and Harry James, the Jitterbug was the dance of the day, and the zoot suit was the latest fashion.

In Los Angeles, California, the zoot suit became the outfit of choice for many young Mexicans and Mexican Americans. The suits came in all different colors. They were often made of wool, but the best were made of sharkskin, a soft, smooth rayon fabric. The cool dudes strutted through the streets in their long jackets, big hats and baggy pants, and showed them off in all the clubs. But the coolest of the cool never danced in their suits, no matter how hot the music got. Instead, a really hip guy stood on the dance floor, straight and tall, lightly holding his girl's arm. She'd dance around him one way until he took her other arm, then she'd dance around him in the other direction and his suit would never get wrinkled—which was the reason he wouldn't dance.

Dancing the Jitterbug

Harry James

Benny Goodman

The Zoot Suit

Nobody is certain where the zoot suit came from. A New York Times article claimed it was invented by Clyde Duncan, a black bus worker from Georgia. It's said he had seen the movie Gone With The Wind and wanted a suit like the character Rhett Butler wore.

Others believed the suit came out of the jazz clubs, along with the word 'zoot.' Zoot meant 'something worn or performed in an extravagant style.' And that's exactly what a zoot suit was.

A zoot suit consisted of high-waisted, baggy-legged pants cuffed tight at the ankles, a long coat with wide lapels and wide padded shoulders, a felt hat – with or without a feather – and pointy shoes. Some people wore a long watch chain that draped down past their knees.

The Zoot Suit was once described as 'a killer-diller coat with a drape shape, reet pleats, and shoulders padded like a lunatic's cell.'

But if the zoot suiters were afraid of wrinkling their suits, and their girl-friends really wanted to dance, there were other guys around. A Naval Reserve **Armory** had recently been built not far from downtown Los Angeles. That meant there were always lots of sailors to dance with not to mention guys from the white and black neighborhoods. In the jazz clubs, girls and music were the great **unifiers**. Jazz clubs were one of the few places where many different groups of people all enjoyed themselves together.

Outside the clubs, things were different. **Segregation** was the way of the day, and people of different ethnic groups usually did not mingle with

Chapter 1: José Gallardo Diaz

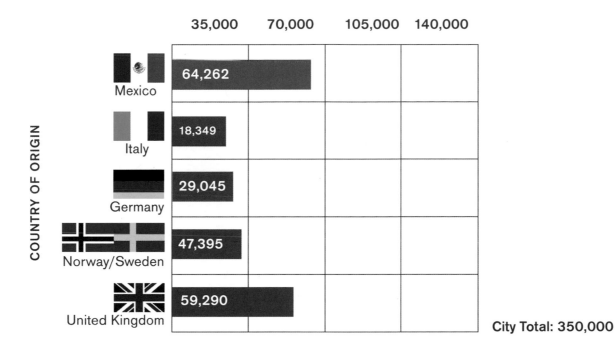

Comparison of Some Foreign White Populations in Los Angeles in 1940

COUNTRY OF ORIGIN	35,000	70,000	105,000	140,000
Mexico	64,262			
Italy	18,349			
Germany	29,045			
Norway/Sweden	47,395			
United Kingdom	59,290			

City Total: 350,000

Mexicans and other Hispanics outnumbered other white immigrant populations in the 1940s.

one another. Many of the white people in Los Angeles—white **'Angelenos'**—frowned on mixing with other races and ethnic groups, and did their best to keep the 'others' as far away as possible.

And there were lots of 'others' in Los Angeles. L.A. was a diverse city. Mexicans had lived there since the city was part of Spain. Whites came with western expansion. Chinese and Japanese communities established themselves there in the 1800s. Italian, Irish and Jewish immigrants moved in around the turn of the twentieth century. After 1910, when the Mexican Revolution began, more Mexicans immigrated to Los Angeles searching for a better life. And in the 1930s, the Depression

airplane parts, and that brought in even more people desperate to escape the hard and hungry Depression days.

All these people lived in segregated neighborhoods, keeping to their own kind. For some, it was a choice. Maybe they didn't speak English so well and liked being near people who spoke the same language. Maybe they were more comfortable in a neighborhood where people were like them.

But most non-whites couldn't have found a place to live outside their neighborhoods if they wanted to. Homes in established white communities weren't sold or rented to non-whites. Even white immigrants were considered 'others' and kept in their own separate neighborhoods.

José's World

This was the world José Gallardo Diaz lived in. His parents, Teodolo and Panfila Diaz, came

brought in **Okies** from the **Dustbowl** states and African Americans hoping to escape the poverty of the south.

When America entered World War II, the aviation industry came to town. Now there were thousands of new jobs making airplanes and

from Durango, Mexico in 1923. Mexico had undergone drought, famine, and ten years of revolution. Each passing day, it had become harder and harder for José's parents to make ends meet. They heard about work in America. They heard about opportunity. They believed America would give them the chance to live a decent life, and like many other Mexican families, they packed up their belongings and **emigrated**.

José was four years old when he arrived in California. By the time he was nine, his parents, who were farm workers, had moved the family to a bunkhouse on the Williams Ranch. The ranch was located just south of Los Angeles, in what is now the city of Bell. José's neighbors were other Mexican and Mexican American families similar to his own.

José grew up like many kids in his community. He lived in a segregated neighborhood, or **barrio**. He went to school and studied hard. And like many children of immigrants growing up in America, José soon became more a part of America than of his native country.

When he finished the eighth grade, he quit school and got a job packing vegetables in a plant. His life wasn't unusual. Many Mexican immigrants worked on farms. They made about 25 cents an hour, or about $100 a month. They

California never has enough water. Most of the state has a short rainy season. It also depends on the snow that melts each spring and flows from the Sierra Nevada Mountains.

While the state is known for a large variety of farm crops, many farmers only can grow their products by storing water in reservoirs.

In the 1940s steam engines, windmills, and pipelines helped distribute water from the reservoirs to the crops.

The irrigation pond or Chavez Reservoir on the Williams Ranch was not fancy, but a little imagination

didn't have steady incomes because much of their work was seasonal. Often, their children quit school so they could work and help out at home.

José worked hard. At the end of each week, he handed his pay check to his parents. On weekends, he went out with his friends. As he got older, going out meant dressing up in his **pegged** pants and heading to a club or party for a night of jazz music and dancing, or maybe just hanging out.

One popular hangout was a local **reservoir** used to **irrigate** the nearby farmland. In the summertime, people from José's neighborhood swam in the Chavez Reservoir because only whites were allowed in the city pools. At night, the

made it seem like a romantic "Sleepy Lagoon."

Sleepy Lagoon
Words by Jack Lawrence,
music by Eric Coates

*A sleepy lagoon, a tropical moon
And two on an island. . .
The fireflies' gleam reflects
in the stream
They sparkle and shimmer
A star from on high falls
out of the sky
And slowly grows dimmer
The leaves from the trees all
dance in the breeze
And float on the ripples. . .
A tropical moon, a sleepy lagoon
And you.*

View on Youtube:
http://www.youtube.com/
watch?v=-syJ-2UPtYw

reservoir became a hangout for the local kids.

Teen-age boys and girls, and young men and women, gathered there to meet friends, or maybe a boy or girl they were interested in. It was out of the way, away from the prying eyes and ears of adults. There was no one to complain about the crowd or the noise, or anything else the kids might be doing. Later, it came to be called the Sleepy Lagoon after a popular song of the time.

On December 7, 1941, the Japanese bombed Pearl Harbor, Hawaii and America found itself at war. José was just turning twenty-two. Like many other men his age, he got caught up in all the excitement. José Diaz, the Mexican, joined the American Army.

José Diaz

José's Last Night

His mother wasn't thrilled. She was proud of her son, but she was scared for him, too. She knew what could happen to men who went off to war, and she didn't want her son to be hurt, or worse. On the weekend before José was to leave for the Army—August 1–2, 1942—his mother sent him to have his picture taken. José had never had his picture taken before. His mother probably wanted a photo to remember him by.

That same weekend, José also was invited to a party. José had his picture taken, and then went to the party. It was at the home of a friend, Eleanor Coronado, who lived near the reservoir.

Jose arrived at a house alive with kids and music. People talked and ate and danced to swing, jazz, and **crooners**. But as the party went on, Louie Encinas—one of the young men at the party—became a problem. There was some shouting and shoving, and Louie was eventually thrown out. Some people at the party said Louie was the only one to be sent packing. Others said several young men were kicked out with him. What actually happened, and why it happened, is unclear.

Around 1:00 a.m., the party began to breakup.

Hank Leyvas and his girlfriend had been attacked and beaten at the Chavez Reservoir.

Gang Leader

Hank Leyvas was one of the older members of the 38th Street Gang. Younger members admired him and were willing to do what he asked—even if it meant fighting other gang members.

According to Eleanor, José left with two friends. Soon after, a group of kids from the 38th Street neighborhood burst in on the party. They were looking for the Downey Boys.

The 38th Street kids and the Downey Boys were both 'gangs' from different nearby neighborhoods. Throughout Los Angeles, there were many neighborhood gangs—groups of kids from the same area who hung out with each other. Adults, and the police, referred to them as gangs, and while some kids were troublemakers

and had run-ins with the police, many were simply kids just hanging out with friends.

On the night of Eleanor's party, a young man named Hank Leyvas, and his girlfriend—both from the 38th Street neighborhood—were beaten up by one of the Downey Boys at the reservoir. Hank and his girlfriend escaped, and then gathered their friends together. They all returned to the reservoir seeking revenge, but by the time they arrived, the Downey Boys were gone.

José Diaz was found lying in the road near the "Sleepy Lagoon."

The 38th Street kids were angry and bent on retaliation. When they heard the sounds of a nearby party, they followed the noise to the home of Eleanor Coronado. They burst in uninvited, thinking the Downey Boys might be there.

The partygoers were surprised by the sudden **intrusion**. They weren't part of either gang, and had no idea what was going on. In only moments, a brawl broke out and several of the partygoers were injured. The 38th Street kids ran off and never did find the Downey Boys. The party broke up and everyone left.

But what happened to José? Where was he?

They found him later, bleeding in the road not far from the reservoir. He had been stabbed twice, and one of his fingers had been broken. His brother rushed him to the hospital, and only moments after they arrived, José was dead.

What had happened? Who had attacked him?

To white Angelenos, the answer was obvious. It had to be Mexican **hoodlums**, those teen-age zoot suiters who ran the streets like they owned them.

But why would white people immediately jump to that conclusion? Why were they so convinced it had to be Mexican teenagers?

In World War II California, there were many reasons.

Chapter 2:
The Road
To Ruin

*President
Franklin D. Roosevelt*

War Time Fears

World War II brought more than jobs and people to Los Angeles. It also brought a lot of fear and worry. Angelenos began to see spies everywhere. But so did many other Americans. And they all put pressure on President Roosevelt to do something to protect them.

President Roosevelt issued Executive Order 9066. This order allowed the Secretary of War and military commanders to declare any part of America as a military area. People could be excluded or detained from these military areas.

Four days later, on February 23, 1942, a Japanese submarine fired on the Ellwood Oil Field near Santa Barbara. Sixteen shells were fired, but most fell short into the ocean or missed their targets. About $1,000 worth of rigging and

*A minor attack on Los Angeles oil equipment on February 23, 1942,
was all that was needed to incite panic.*

Ellwood Oil Field Attack

According to *Parade Magazine*, the attack on the Ellwood Oil Field was an act of revenge. Nishino Kozo, the Commander of a Japanese oil tanker, had stopped at the oil field in the 1930s. As he walked up the beach to be welcomed, he tripped and fell into a prickly-pear cactus. The workers on the site laughed at him as cactus spines were pulled from his behind, embarrassing him.

By 1942, Nishino had become Commander of an Imperial Japanese Navy submarine–the same submarine that fired on the Ellwood Oil Field.

pumping equipment were destroyed. It proved the Japanese were out there, and that an attack on the American mainland was a possibility.

Many white Americans already suspected that every non-white, whether an American citizen or not, could be part of a great conspiracy to defeat the United States. Political and military leaders had begun to limit the rights of Japanese citizens in California.

This attitude alone could have been enough to start any number of racial problems, but Los Angeles experienced one more unusual event.

UFOs?

The very next day, on the evening and early morning of February 24-25, several unidentified flying objects were seen over the city.

Searchlights and Anti-aircraft Guns Comb Sky During Alarm

SEEKING OUT "OBJECT"—Scores of searchlights built a wigwam of light beams over Los Angeles early yesterday morning during the alarm. This picture taken during blackout shows nine beams converging on an "object" in sky in Culver City area. The blobs of light which show at apex of beam angles were made by anti-aircraft shells. See Story on Page 1, Part I.

MARKINGS—Hugh Landis of 1738 W. 43rd Place points to holes made in his car, as it stood in garage, by fragments of anti-aircraft shell that hit near by.

CLOSE ONE—Miss Blanche Sedgwick and niece, Josie Duffy, got up to watch firing and escaped possible injury when shell fragment hit. Mrs. H. G. Landis examines missile.

BEDROOM PIERCED—Here is damage done to bedroom in home of Victor L. Norman at 2036 Easy Ave., Long Beach, when anti-aircraft shrapnel pierced dwelling.

AFTER DUD—Cliff Stingley, air-raid warden (left), and Detective Captain B. B. Carnahan dig for dud.

The Army fired on them with anti-aircraft guns, but nothing was shot down. Angelenos became more and more convinced they would be attacked. They began to suspect anyone that looked, acted, or dressed differently.

Something had to be done to calm fears, and the military acted. On March 2—six days after the UFOs appeared over Los Angeles—General John L. DeWitt issued Proclamation No. I. It declared the Western half of the three Pacific Coast states (California, Oregon, and Washington) and 1/3 of southern Arizona as military areas. *All* persons of Japanese descent would be removed from these areas.

The Battle of Los Angeles

In the top left photo, floodlights are trained on a supposed UFO. The tiny dots are the bursts from the anti-aircraft guns. The object in the middle is the UFO.

The Battle of Los Angeles took place on the night/early morning of February 24-25, 1942. Several UFOs were seen over the city. They were fired upon with anti-aircraft guns. The army claimed it was real. Secretary of the Navy, William Knox, said it was a false alarm due to 'jittery nerves.' While several American lives were lost that night, nothing was shot down out of the sky.

Many people were convinced the object fired upon was a real UFO. The U. S. government took the stand that it was never there. Like all UFO sightings to date, there are many explanations for what people saw. Unfortunately, there is no definitive proof one way or the other.

War-time Internment

Not everyone thought Executive Order 9066 was the right thing to do. FBI Director Herbert Hoover was against it. The First Lady of the United States, Eleanor Roosevelt, tried to convince her husband not to sign it. Missionaries who had served in Japan believed the order only promoted racism.

Eventually, the order would be declared unconstitutional and the government would try to repay Japanese families for their losses. No amount of money would have been enough to make up for the years of suffering they endured.

Flyers went up all over Japanese-American neighborhoods. They ordered residents to prepare to leave their homes.

WESTERN DEFENSE COMMAND AND FOURTH ARMY WARTIME CIVIL CONTROL ADMINISTRATION
Presidio of San Francisco, California
April 1, 1942

INSTRUCTIONS TO ALL PERSONS OF JAPANESE ANCESTRY
Living in the Following Area:

All that portion of the City and County of San Francisco, State of California, lying generally west of the north-south line established by Junipero Serra Boulevard, Worchester Avenue, and Nineteenth Avenue, and lying generally north of the east-west line established by California Street, to the intersection of Market Street, and thence on Market Street to San Francisco Bay.

All Japanese persons, both alien and non-alien, will be evacuated from the above designated area by 12:00 o'clock noon Tuesday, April 7, 1942.

No Japanese person will be permitted to enter or leave the above described area after 8:00 a. m., Thursday, April 2, 1942, without obtaining special permission from the Provost Marshal at the Civil Control Station located at:

1701 Van Ness Avenue
San Francisco, California

The Civil Control Station is equipped to assist the Japanese population affected by this evacuation in the following ways:

1.   Give advice and instructions on the evacuation.
2.   Provide services with respect to the management, leasing, sale, storage or other disposition of most kinds of property including: real estate, business and professional equipment, buildings, household goods, boats, automobiles, livestock, etc.
3.   Provide temporary residence elsewhere for all Japanese in family groups.
4.   Transport persons and a limited amount of clothing and equipment to their new residence, as specified below.

The Following Instructions Must Be Observed:

1.   A responsible member of each family, preferably the head of the family, or the person in whose name most of the property is held, and each individual living alone, will report to the Civil Control Station to receive further instructions. This must be done between 8:00 a. m. and 5:00 p. m., Thursday, April 2, 1942, or between 8:00 a. m. and 5:00 p. m., Friday, April 3, 1942.

Flyers went up all over Little Tokyo—a large Japanese section of Los Angeles. They hung in store windows and on telephone poles, informing the Japanese of their futures. They would be brought to **internment camps** where they would sit out the duration of the war. They could only take what they could carry.

Little Tokyo became a ghost town. Men, women, and even babies were taken away, leaving their homes and most of their belongings behind. They were packed into buses and sent to detainment camps in other parts of the country where they remained until the order to release them came three years later.

What About Fifth Column Spies?

Angelenos believed there were hidden **fifth columns** in the city. During the war, the crime rate in Los Angeles rose and many people blamed it on these unknown spies. They believed these spies incited young people to destroy the American way of life. They also believed the spies worked mostly in the Mexican community.

They believed spies could do the most damage there. The Mexican community already had grievances against white America, and white Angelenos knew this. White Angelenos decided where Mexicans could live, who they could work for and what kinds of jobs they could get, as well as where they could and couldn't go in the city. Mexicans had many reasons not to trust white Americans. Fifth column spies could easily take advantage of this resentment. They could say to the Mexican community, "See how you're being treated. Is this democracy? Is this equality?" If they **agitated** enough, perhaps the Mexican community would rise

The Hidden Fifth Column

The term, 'fifth column' came about during the Spanish Civil War, between 1936–39, just before World War II began. One of the rebel generals, Emilio Mola, gave a broadcast as his army of insurgents approached the city of Madrid. He said the four columns of his army outside the city would be aided by a 'fifth column' inside the city. The fifth column was made up of people inside the city who were unhappy with the government and willing to fight alongside Emilio and his cause.

During World War II, many Americans believed Americans of German, Japanese, and Italian extraction might be fifth columnists. They believed these people were more loyal to their ancestral countries than to America. They thought these people would act as spies and pass on vital information to America's enemies, while causing **sabotage** at home.

up in revolt. And if the government had to deal with revolution or rioting at home, it would not be able to focus whole-heartedly on the war.

While some worried about spies and attacks, farm owners worried about a new agreement between the U. S. and Mexico.

Agricultural Needs

The U. S. had been **deporting** Mexicans throughout the 1930s. As the Depression grew, more and more Americans lost their jobs. On the west coast and in the southwest, Mexicans and Mexican Americans did much of the farm work. The U.S. government felt it should make as many jobs as possible available to "real Americans," so they began what was called Mexican **Repatriation**—sending Mexicans back to Mexico.

Selecting who got sent back was very random. Mexicans who had become, or were born U.S. citizens, were often sent back along with illegal Mexicans. Now, the government reached a new agreement with Mexico. The U.S. would allow Mexicans back into the country. With the war on, many men had joined the Armed Forces and there was a shortage of workers. Mexicans would be allowed to fill that gap. In Los Angeles, this meant hiring them to do farm work.

Many farm owners didn't like the idea. The new agreement said they had to pay these workers higher wages than what they paid current workers. It said they had to pay transportation costs for the workers, to and from Mexico. It also said the workers could not be discriminated against while in America. Abiding by this new agreement meant higher costs for farm owners.

Suddenly, the front pages of many local newspapers blazed with headlines about a Mexican crime spree. They talked about 'Zoot Suit Gangs,' and 'Mexican Goon Squads' running loose in the city. They blamed the sudden increase in crime on young Mexican and Mexican American men.

Some people believed the sudden headlines about Mexican crime were over-exaggerated, or even made up. Mexicans had faced discrimination in Los Angeles for a long time. People in the labor movement believed newspaper owners were working with farm owners to drive the wedge deeper between Mexican and white Angelenos. If Mexicans were seen as criminals, Angelenos wouldn't want any more of them entering Los Angeles County. Perhaps they might even rise up and demand Mexicans be deported again.

ALL THE NEWS ALL THE TIME

LARGEST HOME-DELIVERED CIRCULATION
LARGEST ADVERTISING VOLUME

Los Angeles Times

EQUAL RIGHTS
LIBERTY UNDER THE LAW   TRUE INDUSTRIAL FREEDOM

IN THREE PARTS — 32 PAGES
Part I — GENERAL NEWS — 22 Pages

TIMES OFFICE
202 West First Street

MAdison 2345
The Times Telephone Number

VOL. LXI   CO   MONDAY MORNING, AUGUST 3, 1942.   DAILY, FIVE CENTS

One Killed and 10 Hurt in Boy 'Wars'

Another Victim Feared Drowned in Flare-up of Juvenile Terrorism

One person dead . . . another believed dead . . . 10 others beaten and injured severely was the grisly toll early yesterday as juvenile gang warfare flared anew in Los Angeles County.

Three girl hoodlums joined nine youths in breaking up a birthday party and starting a free-for-all fight in which Jose Diaz, 22, of the Williams Ranch, was beaten to death.

ONE FEARED DROWNED

In still another clash, 11 others attacked five youths at a gravel pit swimming pool in Baldwin Park and chased an unidentified victim into the water, flailing him with tire chains. Capt. Jim Neves and John Keenan, county lifeguards at Hermosa Beach, dragged the pool yesterday but failed to locate the body. The pool is 80 feet deep in some places.

Eleven youths suspected of participating in the gravel pit battle were taken into custody yesterday by Monterey Park police and later brought to the County Jail by Deputies Jack L. O'Dell and Frank G. Hedrick, where they were booked on suspicion of assault with a deadly weapon.

GANG INVADES PARTY

The birthday party, bloody aftermath of which resulted in the death of Diaz and injury to four others, was being held at the Williams Ranch, about a half-mile north of Slauson Ave. in Montebello Township.

Nine boys and three girls, armed with clubs, automobile tools, chains and tire irons came to the house and started a melee with the party guests during which Diaz was beaten to death. Joe Manfredi, 32, of 2608 S. Atlantic Blvd., was beaten so unmercifully that he was in the throes of convulsions when taken to Maywood Hospital.

ONE VICTIM SLASHED

Another victim was Cruz Reyus, 31, of 2236 Gar~ld Ave., who was slashed in the abdomen with a knife. Reyus and Manfredi were later removed to the General Hospital where their condition was described as serious.

Emilio del Gadillo and his daughter, Eleanora Coronado, both of the Williams Ranch, received contusions and abrasions about the head and body.

Five youths were treated at General Hospital for injuries received when they were attacked by the gang near the Consolidated Rock Co.'s gravel pit pool at the east end of Los Angeles St. in Baldwin Park.

They told police that the gangsters drove up in two trucks and

Turn to Page 5, Column 4

Others saw it as more evidence of fifth column spies. They believed these fifth columnists were inciting Mexican and Mexican American youth to rebel and cause problems on the home front. They believed that if the war ever did hit the west coast, these same young people might be convinced to take up arms against America.

The Power of the Press

Whether the sudden headlines were a coincidence or a **conspiracy**, one thing was certain: many Angelenos *did* look at the Mexican and Mexican American community —particularly its young people—as a bad element in the city.

During World War II, America faced all kinds of shortages—food, gas, metals and cloth—and Mexican American teens, some white Angelenos said, just didn't care. Weren't they the ones walking the streets in those outlandish zoot suits made by **black market** tailors? And why was it that whenever a crime occurred, it was always one of those *pachucos*? Those zoot suiters? Why weren't they in uniform like American boys? Didn't they care? Weren't they patriotic?

William Randolph Hearst

What many of these people failed to see, was that most of the people they were complaining about were American boys. They just happened to be of Mexican descent. And many had enlisted in the armed services. Unfortunately, the constant negative headlines coming from the local newspapers made it seem otherwise.

HULL READY TO STEP IN IF ZOOT SUIT RIOTS CONTINUE

LONG BEACH INDEPENDENT

Vol. 5—No. 122—An Interpretive Newspaper   Long Beach, California, Friday, June 11, 1943   241 East Th

Washington, June 10--(TP)--Secretary of State Cordell Hull declared concern over the continued turmoil in Los Angeles between so-called zoot suiters and military personnel. Hull said he learned some of the may have hurt Mexican citize if the Mexican embassy contac envoys, the State Department ready to act.

Tenney Committee: Communists Caused Zoot Suit Riots

Los Angeles--(U.P.)--As the Tenney Committee continues to examine the cause of the recent zoot-s that Communists caused the mayhe

Headlines and news stories were written in ways to inflame readers' attitudes.

Board Member Urges Forced Work Details for Zoot Suiters

San Francisco--(U.P.)--George R. Reilly, along with other members of California's liquor regulations board declared that young zoot suit rioters should be sentenced to labor details ...ough Army ser-

Backlash

The City of Los Angeles decided to act. They appointed a special grand jury to look into Mexican crime. This action prompted the Los Angeles Sheriff's Department to do the same thing. The Sheriff's Department appointed Edward Duran Ayres head of their Foreign Relations Department, and assigned him to look into the matter.

Ayres found there was a lot of discrimination against Mexicans and Mexican Americans in the city. He went on to say that other minorities, particularly the Chinese and the Japanese, faced the same problems, and yet, they seemed to do all right.

WAR EXTRA
Los Angeles Examiner
9 A.M. FINAL

ANGELENOS WITNESS AIR BATTLE

IN THE NEWS

Impossible to Send MacArthur Planes, Roosevelt Asserts

RUSSIANS TRAP 46,000 NAZIS. KILL 12,000

American Plane Reported Downed

HUNT ON FOR SPIES MOINS NIPPON SUB

A photo of enemy Japanese soldiers fighting during World War II. Many Americans feared people of Japanese descent living in America were spies for Japan's Army. It was one of many fears expressed during the war years.

He also claimed Mexicans had inherited 'naturally violent' tendencies from their 'blood-thirsty Aztec' ancestors. He said Mexicans were really Indians, who were really Orientals, and that they didn't have a high regard for human life. He suggested Mexicans would always be a violent people no matter how much training or education they received.

So, when José Diaz was murdered on that weekend of August 1–2 in 1942, Angelenos were primed to blame Mexican American zoot suiters. And in a world of uncontrollable events like food shortages and ration cards, **Axis** armies, invisible fifth columnists, and possible alien invaders, Angelenos were finally faced with something they *could* control. Mexican hoodlums were in plain

FEARS Caused by WAR

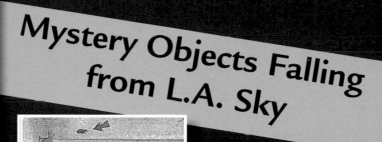

Mystery Objects Falling from L.A. Sky

FIFTH COLUMN

Deep One: Motocycle Officer Bobby Clark reaches into hole caused by a dud shell in a driveway at 1337 Maple St., Santa Monica. The shell was recovered.

Bedroom Pierced: Here is damage done to bedroom in home of Victor L Narman at 2036 Easy Ave., Long Beach, when anti-aircraft shrapnel pierced dwelling.

NEVER BUY RATIONED GOODS WITHOUT RATION STAMPS

NEVER PAY MORE THAN THE LEGAL PRICE

United States Office of Price Administration

IMPORTANT: When you have used your ration, salvage the TIN CANS and WASTE FATS. They are needed to make munitions for our fighting men. Cooperate with your local Salvage Committee.

★ U. S. GOVERNMENT PRINTING OFFICE 1943 16—35570-1

816186 BZ

4

UNITED STATES OF AMERICA
OFFICE OF PRICE ADMINISTRATION

OPA

WAR RATION BOOK FOUR

Issued to _Mary G. Publicixer_
(Print first, middle, and last names)

Complete address _18 Radcliffe_
Arlington Mass.

READ BEFORE SIGNING

In accepting this book, I recognize that it remains the property of the United States Government. I will use it only in the manner and for the purposes authorized by the Office of Price Administration.

Void if Altered _____
(Signature)

It is a criminal offense to violate rationing regulations.

OPA Form R-145   16—35570-1

Pachuco

The word 'pachuco' has meant different things to different people. Some say it came from the Mexican city of Pachuca and meant anyone who came from there. Others say it was slang for anyone who came from the El Paso, Texas area because El Paso was known as the 'El Chuco Town.' According to the Merriam Webster Dictionary it means a young Mexican–American having a taste for flashy clothes and a special **jargon** and usually belonging to a neighborhood gang.

In 1940s L.A., most Angelenos, regardless of ethnicity, interpreted the word exactly as Merriam Webster defined it.

Some of the young men the Los Angeles police arrested after José Diaz's murder.

sight. In fact, the zoot suiters were everywhere. And *they* were subject to American law.

The cries rose up. The streets of L.A. weren't safe! Something had to be done! It was time to clean up the criminal element once and for all!

The police reacted.

Or overreacted.

They swooped down in full force, converging on the barrios. They brought in boys and men and even girls. In no time, the word spread. There had been a fight. A murder. The police were picking everyone up. It was best to stay at home.

The police continued their round-up for two more days, picking up Mexicans at random. When they finally called it quits, hundreds of Mexicans and Mexican Americans had been brought in and charged with all kinds of crimes from loitering to murder.

Henry "Hank" Leyvas was the prime suspect in José Diaz's murder.

Rounding up the Gang

Normally, the police would never have arrested over five hundred people for the murder of a Mexican boy. They considered José's murder to be gang warfare—just one zoot suiter killing another. Any other time, they would have carried on a normal investigation. But the pressure was on to solve this crime and clean up the streets. The police were determined to see that happen.

They zeroed in on Hank Leyvas, a young man from the 38th Street neighborhood, which was several blocks from where José lived. Hank was the young man who had been beaten up with his girlfriend. He was also one of the kids who had crashed Eleanor Coronado's party.

Hank was no stranger to the Los Angeles police. If there was trouble in the barrio, Hank was almost certain to be picked up and questioned. Now, they charged him and twenty-three other young men with crimes ranging from assault to murder.

Clem Peoples

The police questioned the young men relentlessly. They even resorted to violence. Henry Ynostroza, one of the accused, said the police had beaten them up, kicking them and punching them in order to get a confession. He said the police wore gloves so they wouldn't mark their own hands.

Lupe Leyvas, Hank's sister, said that when she went to the police station looking for her brother, an officer opened a door and let her 'see' him. Hank was handcuffed to a chair and was unconscious. He had been badly beaten. The officer told Lupe, "Now you've seen him."

Later, Hank said one of the people who had beaten him was the chief investigator himself, Clem Peoples.

By the time the police finished their investigation, twenty-four young men were under arrest and charged with having a hand in the murder of José Diaz. One was white, two were Mexican, and twenty-one were Mexican American. All of them were members of what the police referred to as 'the 38th Street gang.'

Chapter 2: The Road To Ruin

Chapter 3: The Sleepy Lagoon Murder Trial

Judge Charles W. Fricke

Justice or Sham?

On October 13, 1942, the Sleepy Lagoon murder trial (as the newspapers called it) began. At that time, it was the biggest mass trial in California history. Twenty-four young men were accused of the murder of José Diaz. Two were lucky enough to get separate trials. They were able to hire lawyers who insisted on it. They would go to court after the mass trial ended. The other twenty-two were tried together in an ordeal that lasted three months.

The trial was presided over by Judge Charles W. Fricke, who was sometimes called *San Quentin Fricke.* Judge Fricke was known for sending more people to San Quentin prison than any other California judge. He usually gave harsher sentences to Mexicans than those he gave to whites who committed the same crimes.

The Sleepy Lagoon trial was considered a **farce** by many people. The young men in the case had been held for two months. In all that time, they weren't allowed to have any new clothes or get haircuts.

San Quentin Prison

San Quentin Prison

San Quentin Prison was California's first prison. Originally, it was a ship – the *Waban* – that sat in San Francisco Bay and housed thirty prisoners. These prisoners eventually built the actual prison that would confine them.

By the time of the Sleepy Lagoon murder trial, San Quentin had the reputation of being one of the toughest prisons in the country. It was a maximum security prison which housed the worst criminals and, at that time, legally used torture on its inmates.

The **District Attorney** told their jailer not to allow it. He said they had "a distinctive appearance and for purposes of identification this distinctive appearance should be maintained." So each time they appeared in court, the accused wore the same street clothes they had been wearing when they were arrested. And since their hair was already long because of their duck tail hairstyles, two months later, it was long enough to make them look scruffy and '**disreputable**.'

Another problem was representation. The twenty-two defendants shared just a few lawyers between them. At the trial, they weren't allowed to sit with their attorneys and talk with them. Judge Fricke insisted there was no room for that. Instead, the young men sat alphabetically,

The defendants were not allowed to have clean clothes or haircuts. The prosecuting attorneys wanted them to look like criminals.

directly across from the jury box. They were made to stand up and be identified each and every time their name was mentioned.

As the trial went on, it was brought to the court's attention that these young men had been beaten by police while in custody. But there were no witnesses, and each time a claim was made, the offending officer was brought to the stand to proclaim his innocence.

However, in the case of Hank Leyvas, things were a bit different. His attorney had walked into the room where he had just been beaten, and she had seen his bruised face and his bleeding mouth. She had watched him vomit from the stomach punches he had received. But, once again, Judge Fricke stepped in. If she testified for Hank, he said, she would be disqualified from being his attorney.

The case went on this way for three months. When one of the defendant's lawyers wanted to be sure a witness understood her rights, Judge Fricke told her there wasn't time to explain.

When the defense and the young men all agreed it would be better to have one lawyer, the new attorney, Lester Roth, asked for a short recess to acquaint himself with the case. Judge Fricke refused.

And once again, Edward Duran Ayres entered the picture. Mr. Ayres was head of the Foreign Relations Department of the Los Angeles Sheriff's Department. He was the person who had earlier claimed that Mexicans were a naturally violent people. Now, he was serving as an expert witness for the prosecution. He repeated his theories to the jury, about Mexicans being 'biologically' **predisposed** to violence.

A Tainted Trial

Every day, the all white jury listened to the "facts". And every night, they returned home to read what the newspapers and magazines said about the case. Clem Peoples, the Sheriff's Department's chief investigator on the

Defendants in the "Sleepy Lagoon" murder trial

The twenty-four young men accused in the murder of Jose Diaz did not receive a fair trial. The judge hearing the case, Charles Fricke, was known to be prejudiced against non-whites. He did everything he could to influence the outcome of the trial. He did not allow the defendants to speak with their lawyers. He did not allow their attorneys enough time to prepare the case. Fortunately, the case would be reheard in an **appellate** court.

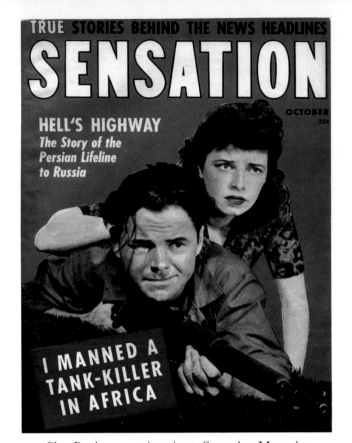

Clem Peoples gave an interview to Sensation Magazine *while the trial was going on. He claimed to know that the young men were guilty of murder and more.*

case—who Hank Leyvas had accused of beating him—gave an interview to *Sensation Magazine*. He claimed that as chief investigator, he knew the young men were guilty of murder and more.

He gave the interview while the trial was still going on. It was very possible some, or all, members of the jury had read it. **Propaganda** about Mexican gangs and zoot suiters could very well have affected their decisions as jurors.

Through it all, the young men continued to

Left to right: Alba Barrios, Frances Silva, and Lorena Encinas were three of the five girls arrested in the Sleepy Lagoon case. One of these girls knew the truth about José Diaz's murder.

people at the party got angry and a short fight broke out. The 38th Street kids left the party, never mentioning José, and returned to the girls at the reservoir, who were still trying to help the injured young man. One of the 38th Street boys admitted hitting José while he lay there, but they all denied doing anything else to him. They said they were not the ones who beat or stabbed him.

Would the Girls Testify?

Now the girls were called by the **prosecution** to testify. There were five of them, but none of them cooperated. When the prosecutor asked them questions, they refused to answer. If they had told what they knew, the outcome of the trial might have been different. Perhaps even the events that followed the trial might not have happened. Because at least one of those girls *did* know the truth about that night. One of them did know what had really happened to José Diaz. Unfortunately, she wasn't telling.

claim their innocence. They had their own version of that fateful night. They said they had gone to the reservoir hoping to find the Downey Boys, who had beaten up Hank and his girlfriend. They didn't find the Downey Boys at the reservoir, but they did find José. Two of the girls spotted him on the ground. He looked like he had been beaten and stabbed.

The girls tried to help José while the boys followed the sounds of the party to Eleanor's house. They thought they might find the Downey Boys there. When they showed up uninvited, the

Members of the Sleepy Lagoon defendants' families such as Hank Leyvas' mother, Guadalupe (center, above), waited for news of the trial's end.

Los Angeles police arrested several girls they believed were connected to José's murder.

Now the headlines rang out again, this time about Mexican and Mexican American girls. The newspapers said they were as bad as the boys, joining them out in the streets and fighting alongside them. It didn't look as though the kids in the 38th Street gang were going to catch a break.

And they didn't.

After three long months and more than 6,000 pages of testimony, the trial ended and the jury came back with their verdicts. Five young men were **acquitted**. Five were **convicted** of **assault** and sentenced to six months to a year in county jail. Nine were convicted of second degree murder and two counts of assault with a deadly weapon. They were given a sentence of five years to life. The last three were convicted of first degree murder and two counts of assault. They were given life sentences.

All charges were dropped against the two boys who were to be tried separately. Maybe the city of Los Angeles was satisfied with the seventeen young men they already had. Maybe they weren't so certain their limited evidence would hold up through a second trial. Maybe the two boys just had better lawyers.

Ventura School for Girls

The girls weren't so lucky. They had not been charged in the case at all, yet they paid a price. Since they had refused to help the prosecution by **incriminating** their friends, they were taken from their families and made wards of the state. Their parents no longer had legal authority over them. The state of California would now make all their decisions for them. And what the state decided to do was to send them to the Ventura School for Girls.

According to historian Elizabeth Escobedo, the Ventura School for Girls had a scary reputation. It was supposed to be so bad that girls in **juvenile hall**, who knew they were being transferred there, would swallow open safety pins the day before. Their hope was that they would injure themselves enough to earn a trip to the infirmary or the hospital instead.

On the day the trial ended, Allied enemies on Axis radio broadcast a message in Spanish to Latin America.

"In Los Angeles, California, the so-called 'City of the Angels,' twelve Mexican boys were found guilty today of a single murder and five others were convicted of assault growing out of the same case. The 360,000 Mexicans of Los Angeles are reported up in arms over this Yankee persecution. The concentration camps of Los Angeles are said to be overflowing with members of the persecuted minority. This is justice for you, as practiced by the 'Good Neighbor,' Uncle Sam, a justice that demands seventeen victims for one crime."

The trial was over, but it would not go away.

Jose 'Chepe' Ruiz

Gus Zamora

Robert Telles

Henry 'Hank' Leyvas

Manuel Delgado

CONVICTED

First Degree Murder

Henry 'Hank' Leyvas, 20, ranch worker.
José 'Chepe' Ruiz, 18.
Robert Telles, 18, defense industry worker.

Second Degree Murder

Manuel Delgado, 19, married, father of two, woodworker. His second child was born the day he entered San Quentin.

John Matuz, 20, just returned from engineering job in Alaska.

Jack Melendez, 21, sworn into Navy before arrest. Received Dishonorable Discharge because of conviction.

Angel Padilla 18, furniture worker.

Ysmel 'Smiles' Parra, 24, married, father of 2 year-old daughter.

Manuel Reyes, 17, arrested a few days before leaving for the Navy.

Victor Rodman Thompson, 21, only white in the group.

Henry Ynostroza, 18, married, father of 1, sole support of his mother and sisters.

Gus Zamora, 21, furniture worker.

ASSAULT

Andrew Acosta
Benny Alvarez
Eugene Carpio
Victor Segobia
Joe Valenzuela

Chapter 4: Riot!

An unlucky victim gets caught on the street.

Racism in Los Angeles

The verdicts did not come as a surprise. Most people, regardless of ethnicity, were pretty certain of what the outcome would be. Many white Angelenos were satisfied that seventeen young Mexicans were now behind bars. That meant there were less of them running around the streets.

The Mexican American community was not satisfied at all. They were certain the 38th Street boys had been **railroaded**. They believed the boys had been found guilty simply because they were of Mexican descent. Here Americans were,

they said, fighting a world war and trying to stop racists like Hitler, yet it was all right to practice racism in their own country.

If relations between the white and Mexican communities were bad before, they were worse now. Feelings of anger and distrust seeped into both communities, particularly among its young people. Small, insignificant things that had once been considered a nuisance, suddenly took on immense proportions. One of those things was a walk downtown.

For those looking for something to do in

Downtown Los Angeles was the place to go for dancing, shows, restaurants, and other entertainments.

L.A., downtown Los Angeles was the place to go. The clubs and dance halls were there. Theaters and restaurants were there. Pool halls and penny arcades were there. The trolley line was there.

Many Mexican immigrants stayed away from downtown. They had spent most of their lives in Mexico and knew they were outsiders in America. They knew they weren't wanted. It wasn't unusual to see signs in stores and restaurants that said 'No Mexicans or dogs allowed.' For many of them, it was just easier to stay home.

But the children of those immigrants didn't care. They weren't like their parents. They were Americans raised in America, and many of them didn't even speak Spanish. They went where they pleased and did what they pleased. Many whites didn't like it, but in most cases, a nasty comment or look was all the young Mexican American would receive.

Sailors Get Involved

Just outside the downtown area, and very close to the Mexican neighborhoods, there was a Naval Reserve Armory. The sailors there also liked to go downtown. To get there, they had to pass through the Mexican neighborhoods. As the sailors walked through the streets, zoot suiters would sometimes toss **barbs** at them, and the sailors would throw their insults back. The sailors tended to resent the zoot suiters for not being in uniform, and the zoot

Naval Reserve Armory at Chavez Ravine

suiters resented being told to fight for a country that treated Hispanics so poorly.

After the Sleepy Lagoon verdicts came down in January, tension between the two groups grew. Things that had been acceptable before the murder—like Mexican American girls dancing with white sailors—were not acceptable after it. And even though some white sailors and Mexican American girls didn't seem to have a problem dating across race lines, it became a thorn in the sides of some of the zoot suiters. Both the zoot suiters and the sailors continuously accused each other of being disrespectful to what they considered 'their' women.

A walk downtown now turned into a dangerous enterprise. Mexican and Mexican American teens were often arrested or roughed up by police if they were downtown after eight p.m. When they returned to their own communities, they were faced with a constant stream of sailors wandering through their neighborhoods. Many felt this was an invasion, of sorts. The Mexican and Mexican American kids could not go where they wanted, but the sailors could go wherever they pleased. They became certain the democracy everyone was supposed to be fighting for didn't exist for them.

The sailors' walk from the Naval Armory

Sailors sometimes sewed pennies into their uniform ties to use as weapons.

The conviction of seventeen young Mexican-Americans was not enough to calm the rioting between "zoot suiters" and sailors.

to downtown Los Angeles and back suddenly changed, too. It turned into a dangerous **gauntlet**. Now, it was no longer just a matter of exchanging put downs. Sailors had to dodge thrown rocks and debris and outrun gangs who might throw punches, instead of insults. As the encounters between the sailors and the zoot suiters turned more dangerous, the sailors became convinced the zoot suiters were nothing but trouble-making thugs.

Throughout the rest of the winter and early spring, clashes between the two groups began to grow in number. Zoot suiters now walked the streets of downtown Los Angeles in long rows, taking up the whole sidewalk so people had to go around them. They'd raise a hand in the air as if about to strike, and laugh as the person flinched. They might even hit a person.

Ready to Fight

Sailors left the Naval Armory prepared for trouble. As part of their uniform, sailors wore a bandana around their necks, called a neckerchief. They would roll up the ends and sew a fistful of pennies into it so it could be used as a weapon if

The Aragon Ballroom was the site of the first clash between the sailors and the zoot suiters.

the need arose.

As the days grew warmer and May rolled around, the first major clash occurred. There was a dance at the Aragon Ballroom in Venice. It was attended mostly by high school kids. When the dance ended and everyone headed outside, the zoot suiters found a mob of sailors and civilians waiting for them. The sailors beat the kids and tore their clothes as the civilians stood by and watched. The zoot suiters had no idea why they were being attacked. Later, they learned a sailor had been stabbed earlier that evening by a zoot suiter. The sailors who had jumped them at the dance were 'getting even' for their friend. They didn't care if the kids were guilty or not. They were dressed in zoot suits so they were fair game.

Later that month, a group of sailors was jumped by a group of zoot suiters. In this case, it was said the sailors had been dating the zoot suiters' girlfriends. The zoot suiters beat up the sailors and, after the fight, the sailors returned to the armory with minor injuries. Their return prompted action from other sailors. They called

Sailors patrol for zoot suiters.

for taxicabs and rode into town, patrolling the area and looking for the zoot suiters who had jumped their fellow servicemen. The sailors never found them.

The Rioting Begins

Then, on Wednesday, June 3, a group of sailors encountered a group of zoot suiters. The story goes that a zoot suiter raised his hand, and a sailor felt threatened and grabbed the zoot suiter's arm. Before anyone knew what happened, punches flew

and men hit and kicked and grappled with one another in a violent free-for-all. But this time, the fighting ended with more than bruises and battered egos. A sailor's jaw was broken and he was knocked unconscious. His friends had to drag him away.

Back at the Naval Armory, the sailors decided enough was enough. Armed with clubs and belts, they descended on downtown Los Angeles. They poured into the streets, grabbing and beating anyone in a zoot suit, and if a zoot suiter couldn't be found, they attacked anyone who looked like they

An angry mob attacks a trolley hoping to find zoot suiters. Newspaper headlines blamed the zoot suiters for the on-going riots.

might be Mexican.

People on the street quickly realized what was happening. Many hurried home to avoid the chance of being beaten. Others were caught unaware. A local movie theater was suddenly invaded. The lights flashed on and a mob of angry sailors charged in. They pulled patrons from their seats, beating men and boys, Mexican Americans, Blacks and Filipinos. Anyone wearing a zoot suit was attacked.

Restaurants and pool halls and penny arcades were invaded. The sailors rampaged through them, finding victims wherever they could. They dragged their victims out to the street, beat them, took their zoot suits, and left them dazed and undressed. Sometimes, they even burned their victims' clothing. In time, the police began to respond. They picked up a few sailors, but did not charge them with any crime. Eventually, they let the sailors go.

The next day, Thursday, June 4th, things grew worse. Emotions ran high as about two hundred sailors hired a squad of taxi cabs and hit the

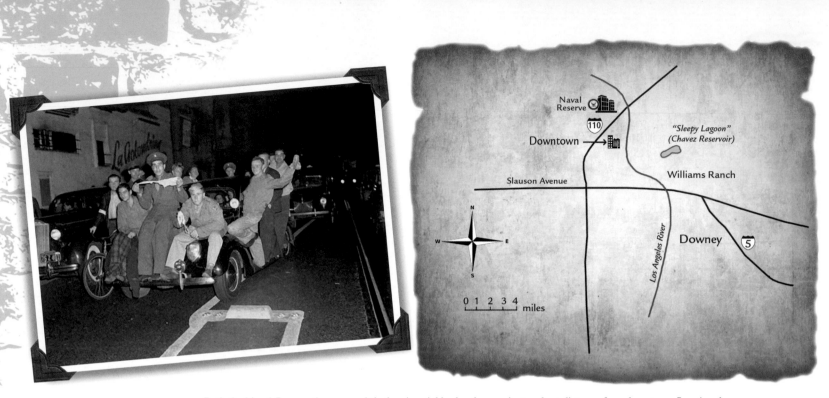

Both the Naval Reserve Armory and the barrio neighborhoods were just a short distance from downtown Los Angeles.

streets of downtown Los Angeles again. Now, they were accompanied by the police. The police followed behind the sailor caravan, waited for them to finish beating their victims, then picked the victims up for vagrancy—wandering the streets without any visible means of support.

Mexican American parents urged their children to stay home. They, themselves, didn't have that luxury, nor did their older children. People still had to go to work. For many, staying off the streets was not an option.

Others had no intention of staying off the street. The zoot suiters were as worked up as the sailors. They had been caught off guard the previous day. On June 4th, they were prepared. They formed large groups of their own and lay in wait in alleyways for the sailors to pass by. One or two of them would stand in the street, waiting to be seen. When the sailors attacked, the others jumped out from their hiding spots and beat the sailors. When a parade of cars stopped at a traffic light, zoot suiters rushed to the cars in the middle and threw punches at the servicemen through the open windows. They ran off and disappeared before the light changed.

Los Angeles Times

IN TIME

Part II — LOCAL NEWS — 20 Pages

TIMES OFFICE
202 West First Street
Los Angeles 53, Calif.

CITY NEWS—EDITORIAL—SOCIETY

MONDAY MORNING, JUNE 7, 1943

CC

VOL. LXII

Wartime Weather
Temperature readings, withheld for 24 hours by wartime restrictions, were reported for June 5 by the Weather Bureau as follows:

By The Way
with BILL HENRY

Why is it that people back East are always talking about the strange folks in California —believe me, you can run into some dillies in the course of a quick trip to New York.

AMBITION—Take Niklina, for instance. This Russian ballerina was the star of Diaghileff's original Ballet Russe and says that she is the only individual in the world who is both a coloratura soprano and a ballet dancer. Her ambition now is to combine the two talents with a swing music and launch a swing soprano ballet technique upon a startled world. Incidentally, she likes the King of Sweden and has danced with the Duke of Windsor but says that his fox trot technique is something that is best forgotten.

Inquiry on Jap Activities Set

Dies Group Here Will Investigate Loyalty of Those Released

How many Southern California Japanese were members of the sinister Black Dragon Society and what percentage of those recently released from war relocation centers are disloyal to the United States will be subjects of inquiry when the special Dies committee on un-American activities opens its hearing here tomorrow.

Representative John M. Costello of Los Angeles, who will act as chairman of the subcommittee, made this disclosure last night in announcing that the hearing, scheduled originally to open today, would be postponed until tomorrow because of the delayed arrival of two members of the committee.

Members on Way

The two Eastern members, Herman P. Eberharter (D.) Pa., and Karl E. Mundt (R.) S.D., are expected to arrive tonight. They are en route here by train.

"Our inquiry will be confined to un-American activities and to extent subversive forces

Zoot Suiters Learn Lesson in Fights With Servicemen

are stripped of clothing by servicemen, most group of youths. They appear at County Jail.

Times Photo

Gangs Stay Off Streets After Dark

Those gamin dandies, the zoot suiters, having learned a great moral lesson from servicemen, mostly sailors, who took over their instruction three days ago, are staying home nights.

With the exception of 61 youths booked in County Jail on misdemeanor charges, wearers of the garish costume that has become a hallmark of juvenile delinquency are apparently "unfrocked."

These were the conclusions reached last night by Capt. David Croushorn, commanding Sheriff's men at the Hall of Justice during night and Capt. Harry Seager, night Chief of Police.

Street Fights Rage

The officers have directed some 200 extra police and 100 deputies who for the last 72 hours maintained vigil at widely scattered points in the eastern sections of the city during a long series of more or less bloody encounters between gangs of zooters and servicemen.

Strife between the two factions arose as a result of beatings of individual sailors by juvenile street bands and, in two cases, assaults on women relatives of servicemen.

These attacks by zooters occurred over a period of several days. The counterattack did not last as long.

None in Sight

Main St. from First to Sixth, California and Temple Sts., Carmelita and Brooklyn and other focuses of habitual zoot-suit congregation all were empty of male zooters last evening, the authorities reported.

On Saturday night, however, an entire truckload of youths —16 of them, all armed with some sort of bludgeon—were arrested at Carmelita and Brooklyn Aves. after they assertedly tried to keep Deputy Sheriffs Foster Kellogg and R. N. Smith from arresting one of their number.

Booked at County Jail

The entire lot was booked in County Jail on riot charges after racing squadrons of officers arrived on the scene.

The suspects said they acquired the truck and were on their way to "have it out" with a bunch of sailors who had sent a bunch at Temple Sts. to accomodate any of the zooters who thought Uncle Sam's fighting men aren't just that.

TWENTY-TWO ZOOT-SUITERS HELD AS YOUTHFUL GANG WAR FLARES

Zoot-suit gang warfare broke out in East Bakersfield Sunday night, police report, with a total of 22 arrests made, 20 of the suspe

of grand theft from the person. They are also wanted in Burbank on burglary charges, Chief Knight

Jr., 89, ny, Dies

pioneer real estate dealer in Southern California. Funeral services will be conducted tomorrow at 2 p.m., at the

Chaplin Plans Legal Reply to Paternity Suit

Charlie Chaplin, pantomime comedian and film producer, today is scheduled to start mapping his legal reply to the charge of a former protege that he is the father of her unborn child.

Since the paternity suit was filed against the actor last Thursday in Superior Court, he has taken no action because his attorney, Loyd Wright, was out of town and did not return until late Friday.

But today he is expected to begin filing his reply.

SUNDAY, JUNE 6, 1943

Sailors Take Matters Into Own Hands; Stage Attacks on Zoot Suit Gangs

Navy men clamped down hard on "zoot suit" gangsters in the Los Angeles area early yesterday.

sailors were all sober, there was no evidence of liquor in the group and all were armed with the

Californians on African

Chief Justice Earl Warren

Earl Warren was born on March 19, 1891, in Los Angeles, California. He was the son of Norwegian immigrants, and grew up in Bakersfield, California. He studied law at the University of California, Berkeley, then entered the U.S. Army as a First Lieutenant in WWI. After the war, he became District Attorney of Alameda County, and from there went on to become Attorney General of California, and then its Governor.

As Governor, Warren supported the Japanese Internment during WW II. In his memoirs, he admitted it may have been a mistake. In 1953, then President Dwight D. Eisenhower appointed him Chief Justice of the United States as a favor for not running against him in the presidential election. Eisenhower assumed he was getting a **conservative** on the **Supreme Court**, but Warren surprised everyone with his **liberal** attitude.

Warren served on the Supreme Court for sixteen years. He presided over such cases as *Brown vs. Board of Education*, which made segregation in schools illegal, and *Miranda vs. Arizona*, which ensured that anyone being interrogated by the police had to be informed of their legal rights first. He was also head of the Warren Commission, named after him, which investigated the assassination of President John F. Kennedy. He died in 1974, in Washington, DC and is buried in Arlington Cemetery.

In just two days, the city was in chaos. A vicious circle of violence had begun, and nobody seemed interested in stopping it.

Many Angelenos were out in the streets, watching the violence, egging the sailors on. Some even took part in the beatings. The police refused to arrest any servicemen, leaving them to be taken care of by the **Shore Patrol**. But the military authorities also stood idly by, expecting the police to stop the madness.

The newspapers made as much of it as they could. For two days, the headlines were all about the riots, mostly praising the sailors and blaming the zoot suiters.

The Community Reacts

The Mexican community held an emergency meeting. Several hundred people showed up. Something had to be done. And fast! They put together a defense committee to help the young people who had been jailed. The committee also did their best to ease people's fears and squash any wild rumors or gossip being spread. They called on California's State Attorney General to talk to the governor, Earl Warren, to set up an investigation into the matter. But they weren't able to stop the fighting.

Now the weekend arrived, and more sailors were on **leave**. The taxi cab caravans grew bigger on Saturday and Sunday, but the sailors' pickings grew slimmer. By the third day of the rioting, even many of the zoot suiters stayed off the streets. With fewer and fewer targets, the sailors began attacking anyone who didn't look white.

As the marauding sailors roamed the streets, a Russian boy stood on the corner with two Mexican American friends. As soon as the boys saw the sailors, the two Mexican American boys ran. The Russian boy didn't. The sailors attacked and beat him.

In another instance, sailors broke the jaw of a twelve year-old boy. He told *Time Magazine*, "So our guys wear tight bottoms on their pants and those bums wear wide bottoms. Who the hell they fighting, Japs or us?"

On the fifth day of the riots, Monday, June 7, the chaos reached its worst point. Rumors

Some people felt that the military police, (Shore Patrol), should handle the rioting sailors instead of city police.

"Vell, Vy Not, Ain't Ve Hoodlums, Too?"

Wearing a zoot suit with its extra material was considered by some to be unpatriotic. A cartoonist compared the zoot suiters to the enemy Axis leaders: left to right, Japan's Tojo, Germany's Hitler, and Italy's Mussolini.

Washington Post Report
Wednesday, June 9, 1943

"At central jail, where spectators jammed the sidewalks and police made no efforts to halt auto loads of servicemen openly cruising in search of zoot-suiters, the youths streamed gladly into the sanctity of the cells after being snatched from bar rooms, pool halls and theaters and stripped of their attire."

and newspaper headlines brought in more servicemen from other military bases across southern California. With the help of taxi drivers, who drove them to Los Angeles for free, they joined the sailors in their campaign against the zoot suiters.

Day Five

As night fell on that fifth day, approximately 5,000 servicemen and civilians roamed the streets of down town Los Angeles. The rioting soon spread from the downtown area into the neighborhoods of East Los Angeles and south to Watts. The angry mobs attacked any male who wasn't white, whether he wore a zoot suit or not.

In the downtown area, they stormed into movie theaters, and invaded trolley cars. They emptied restaurants and clubs. As they spilled into the neighborhoods, they grabbed whoever they could. They beat their victims, took their clothes, and left them humiliated in the streets. And through it all, the police did nothing.

March 22, 1943: A Times cartoon shows zoot-suiters as "solid citizens minding their own bizzness."

Rear Admiral D. W. Bagley

Admiral D. W. Bagley was born on January 8, 1883, in Raleigh, North Carolina. He was a career Navy man who graduated from the Naval Academy in 1904. He rose through the ranks serving on many ships in many capacities. He was at Pearl Harbor during the Japanese Invasion and served as Commander of Battleship Division 2. During the zoot suit riots, he was Commander of the 11th Naval District in San Diego. From there, he went on to command the Western Sea Frontier. He served on the International Defense Board and retired from the Navy in 1946. He died in San Diego on May 24, 1960.

Tuesday, the 8th was more of the same. Fighting in the streets was out of hand, and no end was in sight. Riot fever began to spread. **Vigilantes** in San Diego took to the streets in that city, looking for zoot suiters to beat.

Finally, somebody did something. On Wednesday, the 9th, one week after the rioting started, Rear Admiral D. W. Bagley of the 11th Naval District issued an order. Los Angeles was off limits to military personnel. Only those ordered into the city would be allowed to go there, and any serviceman caught being disorderly would be arrested.

It worked. By June 10, with almost no servicemen walking the streets of downtown Los Angeles, the fighting began to subside.

Food, cloth, shoes, gas, rubber, and other goods were rationed during World War II. Ration coupons were used to guarantee that each family received specific amounts of each item.

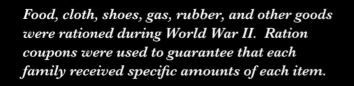

Chapter 5: Freedom?

Mayor Flavor Fletcher Bowron

The Government Steps In

The Rear Admiral's order seemed to set off a chain reaction among public officials. Suddenly, everyone was concerned. But assigning blame, rather than fixing the problem, became the priority.

The **State Department** contacted Los Angeles Mayor, Flavor Fletcher Bowron. They had been contacted by the Mexican **Embassy** who had been contacted by the Mexican Consul in Los Angeles. The Mexican government was on the verge of filing a formal protest to the U. S. government about the riots. They wanted to know what was going on and why, and what was being done to stop it.

The Mayor replied to the State Department saying the riots were not about racism against Mexicans. He claimed they were caused by a few bad apples—gang members who happened to be Mexican American. The Mexican government had nothing to worry about. The trouble was a local matter.

Los Angeles City Councilman Norris Nelson

City Councilman Norris Nelson

"The zoot suit has become a badge of hoodlumism. We prohibit nudism by an ordinance and if we can arrest people for being under-dressed, we can do so for being over-dressed."

Community leaders agreed with the mayor. They blamed the riots on an overall juvenile delinquency problem, not on racism.

Then the City Council suddenly chimed in and made it illegal to wear a zoot suit in public. Anyone caught doing so would be punished with at least thirty days in jail.

The legislature tried to link the riots to fifth columnists and **subversives**. Senator Jack B. Tenney announced he had evidence to prove the riots were caused by "axis-sponsored" agents in America, but he never made that "evidence" public.

Even Eleanor Roosevelt, the wife of then President, Franklin D. Roosevelt, spoke out.

"The question goes deeper than just suits," she wrote. *"It is a racial protest. I have been worried for a long time about the Mexican racial situation. It is a problem with roots going a long way back, and we do not always face these problems as we should."*

Eleanor Roosevelt

The *Los Angeles Times* responded to her comments with a headline that read: "Mrs. Roosevelt Blindly Stirs Race Discord." They also accused her of having **Communist** leanings.

Carey McWilliams, President of the National Lawyers Association in Los Angeles, worked with the Mexican American community on the problems of the riots, as well as the Sleepy Lagoon murder trial. He blamed the riots on the Los Angeles police who, he said, had been harassing the Mexican community for at least eighteen months.

Even the Mexican community was divided on who to blame. Many blamed it on racism, but there were just as many who believed it was the work of fifth column spies. Some blamed it on both. Once more, they pressed California Governor Earl Warren to form an investigation committee to look into the cause of the riots.

At last, the Governor agreed. He formed a Citizen's Committee, and when they finished their investigation, they came to the same conclusion as Eleanor Roosevelt. They found that the riots had happened because of race issues. They concluded that, among other things, a campaign against

Eleanor Roosevelt, 1942

Speaking out on the zoot suit riots was a bold move on Eleanor's part. Until she came along, Presidents' wives were seen and not heard. Voicing her opinions could be seen as voicing the President's opinions. If what she said was unpopular, it could dampen support for her husband and any programs he hoped to put into effect.

Eleanor didn't worry about the consequences. She spoke out on this issue and many more, particularly those concerning civil rights, women, and the poor. Even after she left the White House, she continued working for humanitarian causes for the rest of her life. She led the way for future First Ladies to be more than an ornament on their husbands' arms, and she gave everyday women the courage to speak out and be heard.

Copy of press release sent out by Committee of the Defense of Mexican American Youth:

The Citizens Committee for Defense of Mexican American Youth deplores attacks against the Mexican youth by organized civilian hoodlums and army and navy forces. We feel that incitement for such action comes directly from newspapers which in the last few days have run rampant in their headlines, stories and editorials. It is because of a similar hysteria that 17 Mexican–American boys were convicted in a Los Angeles courtroom filled with prejudice and hatred, six months ago.

Our Committee is now appealing this case in an effort to obtain justice for these boys. We feel that behind the confusion created by the obvious disruptive forces in the last few days, lied a well thought-out Axis plan, carried out most successfully by Axis agents in our midst.

We believe that we owe it first of all to our Nation now locked in a death struggle against Hitlerism to get to the bottom of this outrage and to root out the rats gnawing at our vitals.

In the name of our Good Neighbor Policy, we must get to the source of this outbreak. Our Latin-American neighbots **[sic]** will seriously question our integrity when they learn that we mistreat and terrorize our minorities.

We believe it is imperative that all of our elected representatives, national, state and city, as well as our state law-enforcement agencies get on the job at once to make a thorough investigation and to punish the culprits for their acts of treason.

If we are to win the war and the peace for democracy, we must unite now in a concerted effort to rid ourselves of the Hitler plague on the home front.

Citizens Committee for Defense of Mexican-American Youth

Carey McWilliams was chairman and Alice McGrath was the executive secretary of the CCDMAY

Mexican American teens had been going on for some time, and that it had grown worse after the Sleepy Lagoon murder trial.

Angelenos had come to see Mexican American youth in such a bad light that when the fighting between sailors and the zoot suiters broke out, it was seen as good American boys cleaning up the Los Angeles streets. Many white Angelenos saw it as a good thing.

Of course, not all Angelenos were against the Mexican community. Many white activists, celebrities, and Communists joined with the Mexican community, helping the Mexican Americans' attempts to make things better. Existing friendships between whites and Mexican Americans did not crumble during the riots. And while many whites took part in the riots,

Rita Hayworth

Gene Kelly

Lena Horne

Hattie McDaniel

Anthony Quinn

Vincent Price

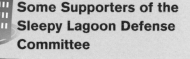

many more of them saw the fighting for the horrible thing it was and stayed home. Unfortunately, few spoke out.

Fortunately, the **posturing** did not last as long as the riots. When it finally ended, the sailors were warned that rioting while in the service could end in jail time, or even a death sentence. By June 14, the riots were over and Rear Admiral Bagley lifted his ban on servicemen entering downtown Los Angeles.

There was no more rioting. Everyone had had enough.

For most people, life in Los Angeles soon settled back into its natural rhythms. But for one group of people, the fighting hadn't ended.

Working to Free the Boys

During the Sleepy Lagoon murder trial, and throughout the riots, the Citizens Committee For The Defense Of Mexican American Youth had done its best to help the 38th Street boys, as well as other young Mexicans arrested during the riots. Now they reformed as the Sleepy Lagoon Defense Committee, and their goal was to get the 38th Street boys out of prison.

Character actor J. Edward Bromberg, (on left) at a Hollywod fundraiser for the CCDMAY at the Mocambo Club on Sunset Boulevard.

The Committee was made up of people from all walks of life. There were activists and educators, lawyers and **unionists**, Communists, intellectuals and celebrities. There were Mexican Americans, other Hispanics, African Americans and white Americans.

The riots had brought the issues of race and discrimination against Mexican Americans out into the light. Before the riots, it was a problem everyone knew existed, but no one talked about. After the riots, it could not be ignored. The Committee used that sudden publicity to focus attention on the 38th Street boys.

They printed pamphlets and wrote articles. They wrote letters to government officials. They demanded that Edward Duran Ayres, head of Foreign Relations at the Los Angeles Sheriff's Department, be fired for making his insulting comments about Mexicans. They raised money for an appeal. Movie stars like Orson Welles, Anthony Quinn, and Rita Hayworth also took up the cause, speaking out on the boys' behalf and attending fund-raising parties.

While all this was going on, the young men convicted of José Diaz' murder were making the best of a bad situation. Stuck in San Quentin

Chepe Ruiz (on left) became featherweight boxing champ at San Quentin

Prison, some of them joined the baseball team or the boxing club, others did war work or helped out in the prison hospital. As their cause became more popular, it brought them at least one privilege. They no longer had to eat prison food. They were given the same food that the prison guards ate, which included steak, pork chops, and ice cream.

The young men also were being encouraged by Alice McGrath, an activist on the Defense Committee, to keep their spirits up. She wrote the boys letters and let them know there were people working hard to get them out of prison. For many of the young men, it was enough to keep them going, and to give them hope that some day, they might actually return home.

Finally, in November, 1943, an appeal was filed, and eleven months later, on October 2, 1944, the Sleepy Lagoon verdicts were overturned. All the defendants were set free and their records were cleared. The young men who had been unjustly imprisoned had spent over two years in custody. Most of it was in a prison for hardened criminals. Hank Leyvas, who police considered to be the ring-leader among the young men, left the Halls of Justice wearing a zoot suit.

The young defendants leave the Hall of Justice as free men.

Officials in Los Angeles still had the option to retry the case. The young men had not been found innocent. They had been released because they had not received a fair trial. But the city of Los Angeles decided to let it go. Perhaps they realized the young men had been railroaded. Perhaps they knew public opinion would be against them. Whatever their reasons, they let the 38th Street "gang" go. The young men were finally free to live normal lives again.

The girls, who had been sent off to the Ventura School for Girls, were not as lucky. They remained in the custody of the California Youth Authority until they turned twenty-one. To this day, none of them have ever spoken out on the murder of José Diaz.

And José?

As of today, his murder is still officially unsolved. Unofficially, the question of what happened that night in August, 1942, has been answered somewhat. If you remember, there was a girl who knew what had happened to José. Her name was Lorena Encinas. She was one of the girls who refused to cooperate with the prosecution and was sent off to the Ventura School for Girls.

Lorena Encinas was determined to protect her younger brother, Louie, even if it meant going to jail.

The Truth About the Murder

Lorena kept her secret for most of her life, but before she died, she confided in her daughter. The reason she had never spoken out about José's murder was because she knew the killer. It was her brother, Louie Encinas, the boy who had been thrown out of Eleanor Coronado's party.

The story Lorena's daughter told was that Louie had not been invited to the party. He had crashed it after it had been going on for some time, and had then been thrown out. He left and found some of his other friends. When José and his two friends left the party, they ran into Louie and his friends and a fight broke out between the two young men. José was stabbed and left in the street. A while later, the 38th Street kids came by and found him.

frustration
racism
anger fear
paranoia
false suicide
patriotism blame
apathy cowardice
rationing jail impulsiveness
war death fifth column spies
discrimination
distrust alien attacks
murder destruction
youth robbery trouble
attack violence
hesitancy
emotions

So if the story is true, we still don't know why Louie attacked José. Perhaps there was already some trouble between them. Perhaps Louie was just so angry at having been thrown out of the party, he would have attacked any of the partygoers. José and Louie, the only people who knew the real answer to that question, are both dead. Louie Encinas, who spent a lifetime in and out of jail, eventually committed suicide during a bank robbery in 1972.

The Sleepy Lagoon murder and the zoot suit riots—sometimes referred to as the Sailor Riots—occurred because of a number of different reasons. Fear and **paranoia**, racism and discrimination, the impulsiveness of youth, apathy, and perhaps even those unseen fifth columnists—they all played a part.

In just a short amount of time—a little over two weeks—they had knocked the entire city of Los Angeles off its feet. Emotions and frustrations held in check for so long burst out in a torrent of anger and violence that might have destroyed a city.

But they didn't.

Friends and family welcomed the young men who were freed when the Sleepy Lagoon verdicts were overturned.

Luckily, there were good people around to see that possibility didn't happen. Not Mexican people, not white people, but American people. People of many different races and backgrounds. Rear Admiral Bagley stood up to end the rioting, and the members of the Sleepy Lagoon Defense Committee, made up of a diverse group of people, stood up for the 38th Street boys and other Mexicans who had gotten caught up in the rioting. And while no sweeping legislation came out of the riots, they did fuel the flames for further activism and the quest for civil rights in the Mexican community.

And the zoot suit?

Like all fashions, it went out of style. But in its day, it was more than a suit. It was a symbol that said:

I am here.
I am somebody, and
I am as good as you.

And in the end, isn't that how we all want to feel?

The Zoot Suit Riots Influence the Arts

In Drama. . .

Historic events have always inspired artists.

Henry Wadsworth Longfellow wrote the narrative poem "Paul Revere's Ride."

Peter Stone and Sherman Edwards' Broadway musical hit, *1776*, tells the story of America's birth as a nation.

Many people don't realize that the folk song called "Fifteen Miles on the Erie Canal" commemorates the waterway that opened in New York in 1825.

The events of the Zoot Suit Riots have inspired works of art as well:

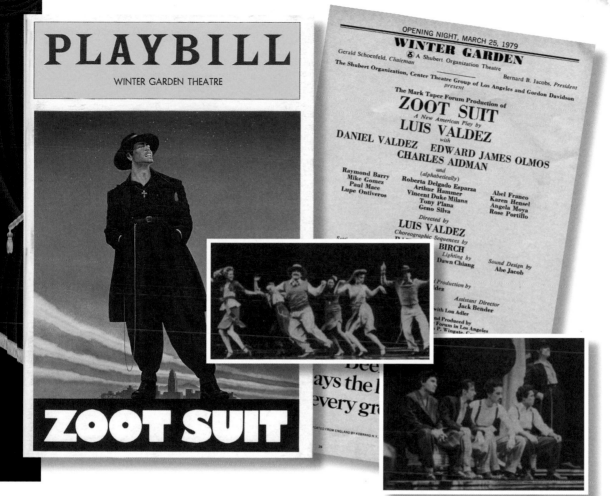

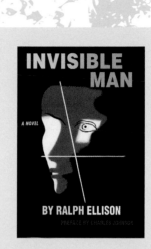

In Literature...

"What about these three boys, coming now along the platform, tall and slender, walking with swinging shoulders in their well-pressed, too-hot-for-summer suits, their collars high and tight about their necks, their identical hats of black cheap felt set upon the crowns of their heads with a severe formality above their conked hair? It was as though I'd never seen their like before: walking slowly, their shoulders swaying, their legs swinging from their hips in trousers that ballooned upward from cuffs fitting snug about their ankles; their coats long and hip-tight with shoulders far too broad to be those of natural western men."

Zoot Suit

A play by Luis Valdez

Luis Valdez wrote a fictionalized version of the Sleepy Lagoon Murder Trial. It was first performed in Los Angeles in 1978. It moved to Broadway in New York City the following year. The play became a film in 1981.

Eight of the Sleepy Lagoon murder defendants found themselves in court again in 1979.

They sued playwright Louis Valdez and others who helped launch the play. They claimed Valdez's play invaded their privacy. The eight men won the decision and were awarded money from the profits of the play. In addition, they would receive 1% of the profits of the film.

In Music. . .

Hey, Pachuco!
by the Royal Crown Review

Summer '43 the man's gunnin' for me

Blue and white mean war tonight

Well when we hit downtown

We start to throw down

We end up doing time

Soon as they've met us

They're out to get us

So I stick with that gang of mine

Listen to the song:
http://www.youtube.com/watch?v=XbtTTxFbNQU

The Zoot Suit Riots Influence the Arts

Zoot Suit Riot—
Cherry Poppin Daddies

Who's that whisperin' in the trees?

It's two sailors and they're on leave

Pipes and chains and swingin' hands

Who's your daddy? Yes I am. . .

Zoot suit riot

(Riot)

Throw back a bottle of beer

Zoot suit riot

(Riot)

Pull a comb through your coal black hair

Zoot suit riot.

(Riot)

Throw back a bottle of beer

Zoot suit riot.

(Riot)

Pull a comb through your coal black hair

Listen to the song:
http://www.youtube.com/watch?v=1IqH3uliwJY

Detroit, Michigan

Across the Nation

While Los Angeles was the center of the Zoot Suit Riots, it was not a lone event. The Zoot Suit riots spread to major cities such as Detroit and New York. Talk of violence created more tension between whites and blacks. Newspapers had spread the reports of the riots across the nation. As in Los Angeles, zoot suiters in other cities were viewed as trouble.

In 1943, black and white Detroit residents felt a lot of stress and strain. At Thomas M. Cooley High School, white students attacked black students wearing zoot suits. Once more, minority students were picked on because of the clothes they wore. The use of extra cloth caused the negative feelings of whites toward these students. Many people believed the attack was a copy of the Los Angeles riots. Like in Los Angeles, sailors had turned against black teens at the Belle Isle beach resort. Rumors about crimes had started this attack. The Detroit Race Riots exploded in June. Three days of riots ended in the deaths of 34 people (25 blacks and 9 whites). Four hundred and thirty people were wounded. Damage to buildings and cars was $2 million.

Harlem, New York

Tensions from the Detroit attack continued into Harlem in New York City. A fight started another wave of riots on August 1, 1943. A black soldier stepped in when a white policeman stopped a black woman at a hotel. The soldier was shot and wounded in the shoulder during the brief struggle. He was taken to a local hospital. A crowd gathered there and when tempers flared, a riot followed. Five blacks were killed, 565 people wounded, and 500 arrests (mostly blacks) were made by the end of August 2. Damage to buildings and cars cost $5 million.

The zoot suits worn by so many people were signs of culture and unity. This clothing also became tied to troubles between many groups.

What About Today?

The story of the Zoot Suit Riots is just one example of the difficulties faced by immigrants. Every American generation has witnessed or experienced forms of racism.

Sometimes, the problem has to do with jobs. Newcomers to the United States often are willing to take any work that is available. When the economy is poor, competition for jobs becomes fierce. Entire groups of people may be blamed for "taking" jobs from American citizens. Irish and Italian immigrants faced these accusations in the early 1800s as factory owners hired those willing to work longer hours for less pay.

In the mid-1800s, Chinese immigrants came to America during the Gold Rush. Later, they were instrumental in building the Transcontinental Railroad. But, in 1882, as jobs again became scarce, President Chester A. Arthur signed the Chinese Exclusion Act. The law was in effect for 60 years and severely limited Chinese immigration.

Sometimes, war incites racism. Japanese-Americans suffered during World War II. Italian-Americans and German-Americans also endured

Today, California firefighters use the old
Naval Armory building as a training facility.

bigotry. Because they were white skinned, it was a bit easier for these groups to hide their backgrounds. Some families even changed their names to more "American-sounding" versions. Mr. Miller might have been born with the last name "Mueller." Mr. Lorenzo might decide to go by the name "Lawrence."

Following the events of Sept. 11, 2001, Arab-Americans faced similar issues. Because the airplane high-jackers had come from Arab nations, many Muslims living in the U.S. and their Amer-ican-born children were taunted or mistreated. The tragedy prompted another version of racism.

Always, racism comes from fear. Fear of the unknown. Fear of misunderstood traditions. Fear of the possible cost of acceptance. Cities and towns wonder if they can afford to assist the new immigrants. How will they provide the newcomers with homes, jobs, or schooling? Will taxes have to be raised to help pay for the new arrivals?

The Zoot Suit Riots show us the high cost of hate.

Timeline

1718	Los Angeles founded as a Spanish city.
1821	Los Angeles becomes a Mexican city.
1850	Los Angeles incorporated as an American city.
1910	Revolution breaks out in Mexico.
1919	December 9, José Gallardo Diaz is born.
1923	Diaz family immigrates to America.
1928	Diaz family moves to a bunkhouse on the Williams Ranch just outside Los Angeles.
1930s	Jazz comes to Los Angeles, along with southern Blacks and Dustbowl refugees. Mexicans are being deported.
1941, December 7	Japanese attack American ships at Pearl Harbor in Oahu, Hawaii.
December 8	U.S. declares war on Japan.
December 11	U.S. declares war on Germany.
1942, February 19	U.S. government rounds up west coast Japanese and Japanese Americans. They are interred in 'detainment' camps until 1945.
February 23	Ellwood oil field is fired upon by Japanese submarine.
February 24 – 25	U.S. Army in Los Angeles fires upon what it deems UFOs.
August 2	José Diaz is murdered.
October 13	Sleepy Lagoon murder trial begins.
1943, January 12	Sleepy Lagoon murder trial ends. Seventeen young men are convicted of having a hand in the death of José Diaz.
February – April	Altercations between zoot suiters and sailors begin to occur regularly.

Timeline continued

1943, May 9	Hundreds of sailors and civilians attack zoot suiters as they exit the Aragon Ballroom
May 31	Fights break out between sailors and Mexican American youths. A sailor is badly wounded.
June 3	About 50 sailors converge on downtown Los Angeles seeking revenge for an attack on sailors that day. They attack anyone they find wearing a zoot suit.
June 4	Sailors return and hunt down zoot suiters in the downtown area.
June 6	Rioting spreads to east L.A. The press is blamed for the continuation of the riots. So, too, are the police, for overreacting to the initial riot.
June 7	Soldiers, sailors and marines come from as far away as San Diego. Taxi drivers offer them free rides to the riots. About 5,000 people gather downtown. Rioting spreads in to the Mexican American neighborhoods.
June 8	Rear Admiral Bagley declares L.A. off-limits to servicemen. The L.A. City Council bans the wearing of zoot suits in public.
June 9	The rioting lessens.
June 14	Admiral Bagley allows sailors to go into L.A. again.
June 16	Eleanor Roosevelt declares the zoot suit riots to be race riots.
November	The Sleepy Lagoon murder trial is appealed.
1944, October 2	The Sleepy Lagoon verdicts are overturned. All the defendants are set free and their records cleared. The girls remain in reform school until they are twenty-one.

Glossary

acquitted (uh KWIT ed) Found not guilty of committing a crime.

agitated (AJ uh tay ted) Stirred up; shook up.

Angelenos (an juhl EE nohz) Residents of the city of Los Angeles.

appellate (uh pe luht) A court able to review lower court cases.

armory (AR mur ee) A building used for storing weapons or training the military.

assault (uh SAWLT) To attack a person in a violent way.

Axis (AK siss) The name given to the combined foreign powers of Japan, Italy, and Germany during World War II that fought against the Allied nations.

barbs (BARBZ) Biting or insulting comments.

barrio (BA ree oh) A neighborhood where Spanish is the common language.

black market (BLAK MAR kit) A way for people to sell goods illegally.

bylines (BYE lynz) The lines at the beginning of newspaper stories or magazine articles that give the authors' names.

communists (COM yuh nistss) People who believe a country should be organized so that all buildings, businesses, etc. are owned by the government and that all profits should be shared equally by its citizens.

conservative (kuhn SUR vuh tiv) A person who is against rash or extreme changes in society.

conspiracy (kuhn SPIHR uh see) A secret plan.

convicted (kuhn VIKT ed) Found guilty of committing a crime.

crooners (KROO nuhrs) Singers who perform soft, often romantic, songs.

deporting (di PORT ing) Exiling, banishing.

disreputable (diss REP yuh tuh buhl) Having a bad reputation. Being known as a criminal or delinquent.

District Attorney (DISS trict uh TUR nee) A lawyer who argues against those charged with a crime and for a particular town or city.

Dust Bowl (DUHST bohl) A name given to an area that suffered from long periods without rain followed by severe dust storms.

embassy (EM buh see) The home and office of an ambassador located in a foreign country.

emigrated (EM uh grayt uhd) Having left one's country of birth in order to live in another country.

farce (FARSS) A ridiculous, laughable situation.

fifth columns (FIFTH KOL uhmz) The secret supporters of a nation's enemy.

gauntlet (GAWNT lit) An old method of warfare in which men with weapons, such as rocks, fists, or clubs stood in two lines and beat a victim who was forced to run between the lines.

hoodlums (HOOD luhmz) Young gangsters or thugs.

incriminating (in KRIM uh nate ing) Showing that someone is guilty of a crime.

internment camps (in TURN muhnt KAMPSS) Areas set up to enclose prisoners of war.

intrusion (in TROO zuhn) Forcing one's way into a situation when one is not invited.

irrigate (IRH uh gate) To provide water for plants.

jargon (JAR guhn) Words used by certain groups or businesses that others might not understand.

juvenile hall (JOO vuh nuhl HAWL) A prison for young people who have been found guilty of committing a crime.

leave (LEEV) Time away from work.

liberal (LIB ur uhl) A person who favors political change.

objectively (uhb JEK tiv lee) In a factual way; not based on emotions.

Okies (OH keez) Immigrants who came to California from other states (such as Oklahoma) to escape the Dust Bowl—a long period of drought in the plains region of the United States during the 1930s and 1940s.

paranoia (pa ruh NOY uh) The unreasonable fear that someone or something is threatening one's safety.

pegged (pants) (PEGD) Pants that were pinned tightly at the ankle.

posturing (POSS chur ing) Taking a certain stand or opinion about an event.

predisposed (pree di SPOZD) Already forming an opinion.

propaganda (prop uh GAN duh) A type of information that is spread to harm a certain group or influence the way people think.

prosecution (pross uh KYOO shuhn) The legal action taken by a court to punish a person found guilty of a crime.

railroaded (RAYL roh did) Convicted of a crime without proper evidence.

repatriation (ree pay tree AY shuhn) Sending people back to the country where they were born.

reservoir (REZ ur vwar) A natural or man-made area for storing water that will be used to water crops.

sabotage (SAB uh tahzh) To deliberately damage property or interfere with the work or actions of another person or group.

segregation (seg ruh GAY shuhn) Keeping people separate from the main group.

sham (SHAM) Something that is fake or false.

shore patrol (SHOR puh TROHL) Military police provided by the Navy to monitor sailors on leave from their ship.

sic (SIC) Used after a misspelling to show that the error was made in the original version of the quotation.

State Department (STATE di PART muhnt) The department of the United States government that deals with foreign affairs.

subversives (suhb VUR sivz) Those who try to overthrow a government.

Supreme Court (suh PREEM CORT) The highest court in the United States. It consists of 9 justices and has the power to overturn judgments made in lower courts.

unifiers (YOO nuh fye urz) Things that bring people or opinions together.

unionists (YOON yuh nistss) Those who belong to a workers' union and organize to push for better working conditions and better wages.

vigilantes (vij uh LAN teez) People who believe they have to right to take matters into their own hands and punish criminals without giving the accused the benefit of a court hearing.

Index

38th Street Gang, 13-14, 28, 33, 55

A

Across the Nation, 66
Acosta, Andrew, 36
agriculture
   Mexican workers, 20-21
Agricultural Needs, 20
Alien invaders, 24
Alverez, Benny, 36
Angelenos, 7, 14, 15, 17, 19, 21
Appellate Court, 32
Aragon Ballroom, 40, 41
Arthur, President Chester A., 68
assault convicts, 36
aviation industry, 8
Axis armies, 24, 48
   radio broadcast, 35
Ayres, Edward Duran, 23, 32, 56

B

Backlash, 23
Bagley, Rear Admiral D.W., 49, 55, 61
barrio, 9, 26
Barrios, Alba, 33
Battle of Los Angeles, 17
Belle Isle Beach Resort, 66
black market, 22, 24
Bowron, Mayor Flavor Flecher, 51
boxing, 57
Bromberg, J. Edward, 55-56
Butler, Rhett, 6

C

Carpio, Eugene, 36
cartoon, 48-49
celebrities, 55
Chavez Reservoir, 10. *See also* Sleepy
 Lagoon and Hank Leyvas, 13
Chinese Exclusion Act, 68
Citizens Committee for Defense of
Mexican American Youth, 52-53
   Press Release, 53

Coates, Eric, 11
Cool Cats, 5
Community Reacts, 46
convicted, list of, 36
Coronado, Eleanor
   Prelude to Murder, 12-14
Coulouris, George, 55

D

dancing, 5
Day Five, 48
Defendants in the "Sleepy Lagoon"
   Murder Trial, **32**
   list of convicted, 36
Delgado, Manuel, 36
Democracy, 39
Detroit Race Riot of 1943, 66
Dewitt, General John L., 17
Diaz, Jose Gallardo, 5, 8–11, 58
   murder of, 12-14
   Teodolo and Panfila, 8-9
discrimination, 6-9, 23, 38, 60. *See also*
   Sailors Role in Segregation;
Downey Boys, 12-13
Duncan, Clyde, 6
Dustbowl, 8

E

Edwards, Sherman, 62
Eleanor Roosevelt, 1942, 53
Ellwood Oil Field Attack, 15-16
emigration, 9
Escobedo, Elizabeth, 35
Encinas, Lorena, 38, 58-59
   Louie, 12, 59-60
Executive Order 9066, 15, 18

F

Fears Caused by War, 25
female defendants, 32-35
Fifth Column, 19, 21, 24–25, 52
First Degree Murder Convicts, 36

Foreign Relations Department, 23, 32
Fricke, Judge Charles W., 29-31

G

Gang Leader, 13
Garfield, John, 55
Glossary, 70-71
Goodman, Benny, 5
Gone with the Wind, 6
Government Steps In, 51
graph (Comparison of Some Foreign
   White Populations in LA in 1940), 7
Great Depression, 8, 20

H

Hall of Justice, 58
Harlem, 67
Hayworth, Rita, 55-56
Hearst, William Randolph, 22
Hidden Fifth Column, 19
Hispanics in World War II, 12
Hilter, 48
Holton, Karl, 27
Hoover, Herbert, 18
Horn, Lena, 55
Housing, Mexican American, 9

I

Immigration of
   Chinese, 7, 66
   Japanese, 7
   Jewish, 7
   historical, 66-67
   Irish, 7
   Mexican, 7
immigration reform protest, 66-69
In Literature, 63
internment of Japanese, 17-18, 46
   Camps, 18
Introduction, 4

J

James, Harry, 5
Japanese Internment Notification, 18

jazz, 5-6
Jeffries, Herb, 55
Jitterbug, 5
Jose Diaz: Cold Case, 59
Jose's Last Night, 12
Jose's World, 8
Justice or Sham?, 29

K

Kazan, Elia, 55
Kelly, Gene, 55
Knox, William, 17
Kozo, Nishino, 16

L

Lawrence, Jack, 11
Leyvas, Guadalupe (mother), 34
Leyvas, Hank, 13, 36, 57
    arrest of, 27-28
    trial of, 31
Leyvas, Lupe, 28
Little Tokyo, 18
Longfellow, Henry Wadsworth, 62
Los Angeles, 38
    and World War II, 15
    aviation industry, 8
    downtown, 38, 42-48
    Ellwood Oil Field, 15
    Little Tokyo, 18
    Sheriff Department, 23
Lyrics. *See Songs*

M

Maps
    Ellwood Oil Field, 16
    Los Angeles, site of riot, 44
mass trial, 29
Matuz, John, 36
McDaniel, Hattie, 55
McGrath, Alice, 54, 57

McWilliams, Carey, 53–54
Melendez, Jack, 36
Mexican
    farm workers, 9, 20-21
    history of, 9
    immigrants, 9
    reaction to riot, 46
Mexican Embassy, 51
Mexican Juvenile Crime in LA, 1942, 27
Mexican Revolution, 7
mob, 41, 43-44, 48
murder of Jose Diaz
    prelude to, 12-14
    mystery solved, 59
    resolution of, 58–59, 60
Mussolini, 48

N

Naval Armory, 38, 39–40, 42
Naval & Marine Corp. Reserve Center, 38-39, 42
    plaque, 67
neckerchief, 40
Need for Reservoir, 10
Nelson, Norris, 52
newspaper headlines, 23, 46
    LA Times, 17, 21, 45
    miscellaneous, 45
Washington Post, 48

O

Oakies, 8

P

Pachuco, 22, 26
Padilla, Angel, 36
Parra, Ysmel 'Smiles', 36
"Paul Revere's Ride," 62
Pearl Harbor, bombing of, 11
Peoples, Clem, 28, 32
plays
    1776, 62

Zoot Suit, 63
police
    blame, 53
    response, 43-44, 46
    round-up, 26-27, 34
    and violence, 28, 39
Power of the Press, 22
prelude to murder, 12-14
prelude to riot, 26-27, 37-39
Price, Vincent, 55
Proclamation No. 1, 17

Q

Quinn, Anthony, 55- 56

R

Racism, 52-54
    Arab-American, 67
    definition of, 67
    examples of, 8
    Hidden Fifth Column, 19
    Japanese, 16, 18 66-67
    newspapers, 21. *See also* Yellow Journalism
Racism in Los Angeles, 37
ration cards, food & gas, 25, 50
Ready to Fight, 40
Rear Admiral D.W. Bagley, 49
repatriation, 20
reservoir, 10
revenge, 41-44
Reyes, Manuel, 36
riot
    Detroit, 66
    blame for, 51-53
    destruction from, 42
    Harlem, 67
    Mexican Reaction to Riot, 46
    police response to, 42-44
    prelude to, 26-27, 37-39

subsiding, 49

violence during, 42-44, 47

Rioting Begins, 42

Rodgers, Jr. Mrs. Will, 55

Roosevelt, Eleanor, 18, 52-53

Roosevelt, Franklin D., 15

Roth, Lester, 32

Rounding up the Gang, 27, 41

Royal Crown Review, 64

Ruiz, Jose, 36, 57

S

sailor

patroling, 42-43

prelude to riot, 37-42

punishment, 49, 55

uniform, 40-41

weapons, 40, 42

Sailors Get Involved, 38

San Quentin Prison, 30

convicts life, 57

second Degree Murder Convicts, 36

Segobia, Victor, 36

segregation, 6-9, 46

barrio, 9

downtown Los Angeles, 38

Sensation Magazine, 32

September 11, 2001, 67

Sharkskin, 5

Sierra Nevada Mountains, 10

Silva, Frances, 33

Sleepy Lagoon

history of, 11

song, 11

Sleepy Lagoon Defense Committee, 55-57, 61

list of celebrities, 55

Sleepy Lagoon Murder Trial, 29, 53

defendants, 31, 34, 36

Defense Committee, 55-57

female defendants, 33-35, 58

mistreatment during, 30-32

propaganda about, 32, 34

testimonies, 32

verdict, 34-36, 57

Some Supporters of the Sleepy Lagoon Defense Committee, 55

Songs

"Cherry Poppin Daddies," 65

"Fifteen Miles on the Erie Canal," 62

"Hey, Pachuco!," 64

"Sleepy Lagoon," 11

Spanish Civil War, 19

spies, 19

Stone, Peter, 62

swing dancers, 5

T

Tainted Trial, 32

taxicabs' role in riot, 42-43, 47-48

Telles, Robert, 36

Tenny, Senator Jack B., 52

Thomas M. Cooley High School, 66

Thompson, Victor Rodman, 36

Time Magazine, 47

Timeline of Zoot Suit Riots, 68-69

Truth About the Murder, 59

U

UFOS?, 16-17

Battle of Los Angeles, 17

V

Valdez, Louis, 63

Valenzuela, Joe, 36

Ventura School for Girls, 35, 58

verdict, 34-35, 57

violence, 37, 40

during riot, 43, 47-48

revenge, 41

W

Waban Prison Ship, 30

War Time Fears, 15

War Time Internment, 18

Warren, Chief Justice Earl, 46, 53

Washington Post Report, 48

Welles, Orson, 55-56

What About Fifth Column Spies?, 19

What About Today?, 66

William Randolph Hearst & Yellow Journalism, 22

Williams Ranch, 9-10

word cloud, 60

Working to Free the Boys, 55

World War II, 8, 15-19

military action, 24

Executive Order 9066, 15, 18

shortages during, 22

Would the Girls Testify?, 33

Y

Yellow Journalism, 22-24

examples of, 23

Hearst, William Randolph, 22

Ynostroza, Henry, 28, 36

Z

Zamora, Gus, 36

zoot suit. *See also* Across the Nation

blame, 51-52

Black Market, 22

conviction, 41, 61

description of, 5-6

history of, 6, 61

In Literature, 63

gangs, 21

zoot suit play, 63

Zoot Suit Riots Influence the Arts, 62-65

Photo credits

Page 5 (top) National Hand Dance Association; (middle) ASB; (bottom) Library of Congress

Page 6 © Bettmann/CORBIS

Pages 8-10 (left) National Archives

Page 13 UCLA Charles E. Young Research Library Department of Special Collections, Los Angeles Times Photographic Archives

Page 15 Courtesy of Franklin D. Roosevelt Presidential Library & Museum

Page 17 Copyright ©1943 Los Angeles Times. Reproduced with Permission.

Page 18 National Archives

Page 20 Library of Congress

Page 21 Copyright ©1943 Los Angeles Times. Reproduced with Permission.

Page 22 Library of Congress

Page 24 National Archives

Page 25 (left and middle) Copyright ©1943 Los Angeles Times. Reproduced with Permission; (bottom) Courtesy of Mary Brown and Sister Ann Publicover

Page 26 UCLA Charles E. Young Research Library Department of Special Collections, Los Angeles Times Photographic Archives

Page 27 CarlesVinyas

Page 28 (bottom) Herald-Examiner Collection/Los Angeles Public Library

Page 29 Iwitness.com

Page 30 Courtesy of CDCR Office of Public and Employee Communications

Page 31 UCLA Charles E. Young Research Library Department of Special Collections, Los Angeles Times Photographic Archives

Page 32 (left) Herald-Examiner Collection/Los Angeles Public Library; (right) Apprentice Shop Books

Page 33 Herald-Examiner Collection/Los Angeles Public Library

Page 34 (left) UCLA Charles E. Young Research Library Department of Special Collections, Los Angeles Times Photographic Archives

34 Laura Aguayo/Pinterest.com

Pages 35 & 37 UCLA Charles E. Young Research Library Department of Special Collections, Los Angeles Times Photographic Archives

Page 38 Courtesy of http://vintage.es

Page 39 National Archives

Page 40 (left) Apprentice Shop Books; (right) Santa Monica History Museum

Page 41 Library of Congress

Page 42 Corbis/Bettman

Page 43 Associated Press

Page 44 CarlesVinyas

Page 45 (bottom) Copyright © 1943 Los Angeles Times. Reprinted with Permission.

(top) Courtesy of Newspapers.com

Page 46 Wikipedia Commons

Page 48 Dorman H. Smith

Page 49 (left) Copyright © 1943 Los Angeles Times. Reprinted with Permission.; (right) Wikipedia Commons

Page 50 National Archives

Page 51 Housing Authority of the City of Los Angeles/ Southern California Library for Social Studies and Research

Page 52 Wikipedia Commons

Page 53 Library of Congress

Pages 54, 56-58, 61 UCLA Charles E. Young Research Library Department of Special Collections, Los Angeles Times Photographic Archives

Page 62 (left) UCLA Charles E. Young Research Library Department of Special Collections, Los Angeles Times Photographic Archives; (right) Apprentice Shop Books

Page 63 (left) Apprentice Shop Books; (right) Random House

Page 66 (left) Corbis/Bettman; (right) Ninian Reid/ Flickr

Page 67 Library of Congress

Page 68 Library of Congress

Page 69 (left) American Freedom Party; (right) James Ehrhardt

Illustrations credits

Cover, title page; pages 7, 10-11, 12, 14, 16, 19, 23, 25 (top right), 28 (top), 36, 44, 47, 55, 59, 60, 62, 63 (right side), 64-65 by © Lisa Greenleaf

Special Thanks

Kyle Drayer, cover model

I am here.
I am somebody, and I am as good as you.

About Author

Barbara J. Turner is the author of *A Little Bit of Rob*, and *Out and About at the Orchestra,* and is also a contributing author to Apprentice Shop Book's *America's Notable Women Series*. She has always been interested in history—particularly in the story behind the story—and in what makes people do the things they do. She's found that history is more often made by ordinary people doing what they believe is right, rather than extraordinary people doing extraordinary things. She, herself, is an ordinary person, writing for ordinary kids who might someday, perhaps, make history themselves.

About Illustrator

Lisa Greenleaf is an award-winning illustrator and author. Her images and stories have graced many children's books including, *John Greenleaf Whittier's The Barefoot Boy, Feathers & Trumpets A Story of Hildegard of Bingen, When Rivers Burned: The Earth Day Story* and the *America's Notable Women Series*.

Lisa continues to follow her passion for art and design and has a successful design business, *Greenleaf Design Studio*. She has been featured in the news, TV, radio, art shows and book events. Lisa is an accomplished motivational speaker and has made many presentations at events and programs, sharing her stories, anecdotes, inspirational messages, music and tools that she incorporates throughout her work and daily life. www.Lisagreenleaf.com

Zoot Suit Summary

Should clothing capture the spirit of a culture, define people, or make them targets? In the case of a zoot suit, wearing one during World War II meant all three.

The freedom of the 40's—night clubs, jazz music, swing dancing—masks the underlying racial tensions of the era. Wearing zoot suits was a way to display style and culture but ended up making Mexican Americans targets. Fueled by World War II paranoia, tensions rose to an unforgiving point in June 1943 Los Angeles when wearing a zoot suit meant you were likely to become a victim. Capturing the racial tension of the period, *Zoot Suit Riots* describes the turbulent events that divided communities, pitted servicemen against immigrants, and shut down a city.